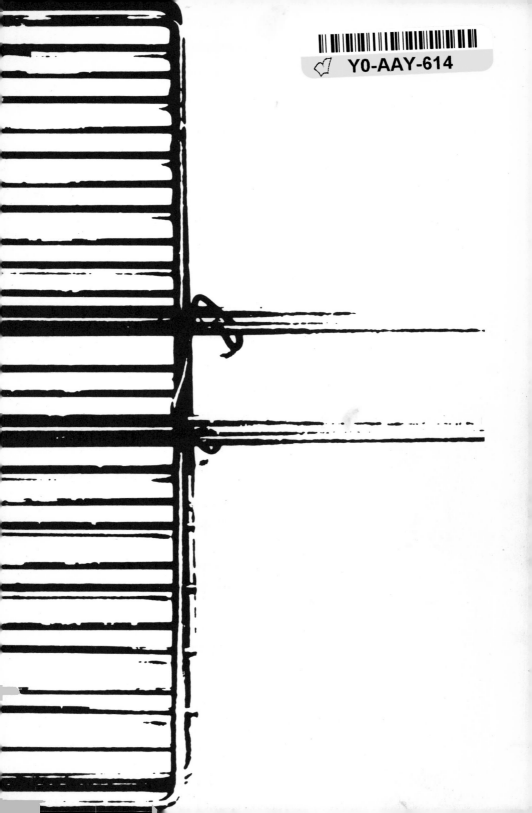

BARBECUE COOKBOOK

ELIZABETH SEWELL

Top to Bottom:
Prawn Kebabs
Chicken Liver Appetizers
Mushroom Buttons

Previous Page:
Herbed Grilled Fish

Published by
Paul Hamlyn Pty. Ltd.
176 South Creek Road,
Dee Why West, New South Wales, 2099.
© Copyright Paul Hamlyn Pty. Ltd. 1971
ISBN 0 600 07019 0
First Published 1971
Printed by Lee Fung

Designed by
Catherine Higson

PRINTED IN HONG KONG

Barbecue Cookbook

by
Elizabeth Sewell
photography and art direction
Norman Nicholls
food for photography
Anne Marshall
Elizabeth Sewell

PAUL HAMLYN
London, Sydney, New York, Toronto

Introduction

The Barbecue Cookbook covers all aspects of barbecuing. It will appeal to all those who like the casual, outdoor way of life.

Barbecues are a good idea for everyday family meals and for parties when entertaining a large number of people. With a little organization, the food can be prepared in advance and everyone can relax together and have fun. Children will love helping with the cooking. All the dishes in this book can be actually cooked on a barbecue. There are limitless ideas for delicious meals, they vary from simple family fare to more sophisticated ideas for party food.

Pack up your portable barbecue, prepare and collect your food and go off into the country for an enjoyable relaxing day. Instead of serving barbecued chops or steaks once again, why not try barbecuing a chicken or freshly caught fish?

There are recipes for vegetables, salads and breads which are perfect accompaniments. There are also sauces, marinades and relishes which will add flavour to any barbecued food.

Children and teenagers love barbecue parties. Serve hamburgers, frankfurters or sausages in crusty rolls or ask the children to make up their own kebabs. There are recipes for tasty desserts to follow.

For a more festive occasion when entertaining a large number of people, barbecue a lamb or sucking pig. It is surprisingly easy and both are delicious to eat.

There is information here which will help you build and light your next barbecue fire and it is not difficult with these helpful hints.

The Barbecue Cookbook will certainly be a valuable addition to your collection of recipe books. Happy barbecuing!

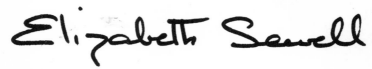

Contents

Weights and Measures

The weights and fluid measures used throughout this book refer to those of THE STANDARDS ASSOCIATION OF AUSTRALIA. All spoon measurements are level.
A good set of scales, a graduated Australian Standard measuring cup and a set of Australian Standard measuring spoons will be most helpful. These are available at leading hardware stores.

The Australian Standard measuring cup has a capacity of 8 fluid ounces.
The Australian Standard tablespoon has a capacity of 20 millilitres.
The Australian Standard teaspoon has a capacity of 5 millilitres.

IMPORTANT WEIGHTS AND MEASURES
AMERICAN weights and measures are the same except for the tablespoon.
Housewives in AMERICA and CANADA using this book should remember that the AUSTRALIAN standard measuring tablespoon has a capacity of 20 millilitres, whereas the AMERICAN/CANADIAN standard measuring tablespoon has a capacity of 15 millilitres, therefore all tablespoon measures should be taken generously in AMERICA and CANADA.

Appetizers

Start your next barbecue party with a delicious appetizer. A tasty morsel of food with which to begin the meal. Seafood kebabs, flavoursome meatballs and grilled grapefruit, all can be cooked successfully on a barbecue. Plan your next dinner menu in advance and the entire meal can be cooked and eaten out of doors.

When serving appetizers for a large number of people, make sure they are bite size, serve on large plates, place a cocktail stick in each and supply plenty of serviettes. Your party will be off to a good start.

Baked Grapefruit

For each serving:

$\frac{1}{2}$ **grapefruit**
1 tablespoon ($\frac{1}{2}$ oz) brown sugar
1 tablespoon sherry or rum
$\frac{1}{4}$ **oz butter**

Loosen grapefruit from skin with a small sharp knife.
Remove centre core and separate segments. Sprinkle fruit
with brown sugar and sherry and dot with butter.
Barbecue over hot coals for approximately 20 minutes or
until grapefruit is warm through.
Note: To serve flaming, omit sherry and when grapefruit is
warm, add 1 tablespoon rum, warm and ignite. Serve
immediately.

Baked Oysters

SERVES: 4-6

24 oysters
Marinade:
3 tablespoons oil
3 tablespoons lemon juice
½ teaspoon salt
freshly ground pepper
1 teaspoon dry mustard
½ teaspoon curry powder

Remove oysters from shells, place in marinade for approximately 30 minutes, turn once. Replace oysters in shells and pour a little of the marinade into each shell.
Barbecue oysters over hot coals for approximately 10-15 minutes or until oysters are cooked.
Serve immediately.
Marinade: Combine all ingredients and mix together thoroughly.

Barbecued Meatballs

SERVES: 6

8 oz finely minced steak
1 egg
1 teaspoon plain flour
1 tablespoon grated onion
$\frac{3}{4}$ teaspoon salt
freshly ground pepper
2 oz butter or margarine

Place all ingredients except butter in a mixing bowl and
mix together thoroughly. Shape into 1-inch balls.
Heat butter in a heavy based frying pan or skillet and cook
meatballs on barbecue over hot coals for approximately
20 minutes or until golden brown. Shake pan frequently
to make sure meatballs are cooked on all sides.
Serve on cocktail sticks with Barbecue Sauce (see page 95)
or Fresh Chutney (see page 102).

Grilled Ham and Cheese Rolls

For each serving:

1 slice ham
French mustard
1 slice processed Cheddar cheese
$\frac{1}{4}$ oz butter or margarine, melted

Spread ham thinly with French mustard and place a slice
of cheese on top. Roll up and secure with cocktail sticks.
Brush with butter and barbecue over medium hot coals for
approximately 10 minutes, turn frequently and brush once
or twice with butter while cooking. When ham is lightly
browned and cheese begins to melt, remove cocktail sticks
and serve immediately.

11

Chicken Liver Appetizers

MAKES: 16

1 x 15 oz can artichoke hearts
French dressing (see page105)
1 lb chicken livers
8 oz bacon rashers

Drain artichoke hearts, cut in halves, and marinate in French dressing for several hours. Wash chicken livers thoroughly and trim off threads and gall. Remove rind from bacon and cut rashers in halves.
Wrap chicken livers in pieces of bacon and secure with cocktail sticks. Spear half an artichoke heart onto the end of each cocktail stick.
Barbecue over hot coals for approximately 7-10 minutes or until chicken livers are cooked and bacon is lightly brown and crisp.
Variation: Small mushrooms, cleaned and trimmed, may replace the artichoke hearts.

Mushroom Buttons

Wash small mushrooms and remove stalks. Fill mushroom caps with pâté.
Melt butter in a heavy based frying pan or skillet and cook mushrooms over hot coals for approximately 10 minutes or until tender. Baste frequently with butter while cooking.
Fry small bacon rolls in the pan at the same time, until crisp and brown and serve with the mushrooms.

Prawn Kebabs

SERVES : 4

1 lb green prawns (or shrimp)
6-8 rashers bacon
2 oz butter or margarine, melted
$\frac{1}{4}$ cup lemon juice

Shell and devein prawns. Remove rind from bacon and cut rashers in halves or thirds. Wrap each prawn in a piece of bacon and thread onto bamboo skewers. Combine melted butter and lemon juice and brush over kebabs.
Barbecue kebabs over hot coals for approximately 10-15 minutes or until prawns are cooked and bacon is lightly brown and crisp. Turn frequently while cooking and before serving, brush again with the melted butter and lemon juice. Pour any remaining butter into a small bowl or jug and serve with the kebabs.

Scallop and Fruit Kebabs

Alternate scallops and pieces of firm banana or peach onto skewers. Brush with combined melted butter and lemon juice.
Barbecue over hot coals for approximately 15-20 minutes or until scallops are tender. Be careful not to overcook scallops as they will become tough. Brush kebabs with melted butter and lemon juice again before serving.
Variation: Wrap the pieces of banana or peach in bacon before placing on skewers with scallops. Replace scallops with bite size pieces of any available fresh fish.

Barbecued Meat

Nothing could be more tantalizing than the smell of barbecued meat—steaks, chops or tasty spareribs. Marinated beforehand, basted with your favourite sauce, all can be truly delicious. Barbecue individual pieces of meat or barbecue a joint whole, carve and serve with vegetables or salads. Barbecued meat is much tastier than the same meat cooked in an oven.

The art of barbecuing meat is to keep the juices in, not use them to feed the fire. Keep the meat a reasonable distance from the glowing coals and turn every few minutes. This keeps the juices running back and forth in the meat and away from the heat. You will find the meat is juicy when cooked this way. Select a variety of mustards, relishes and sauces to accompany the barbecued meat.

Grilled meat, casseroles and foil wrapped chops are just a few of the delicious dishes to choose from.

14

Grilled Lamb Chops and Cutlets

Choose leg, chump, loin, rib, forequarter or shoulder chops
(or leg steak, sirloin, loin, rib, blade or arm chops).
Allow 1-2 chops for each person.
Trim excess fat from chops and barbecue over medium hot
coals for approximately 10-15 minutes or until meat is
tender and evenly brown on both sides.
While barbecuing, chops may be basted with favourite
marinade or barbecue sauce.
If preferred, cook a loin of lamb whole. Ask your butcher to
cut through the bone only, so that the chops can be cut
with a knife when cooked.
Trim excess fat from loin and, turning frequently, barbecue
over medium hot coals for approximately 45 minutes or
until cooked as desired. By turning frequently, the meat
juices will run up and down inside the meat and it will
retain more moisture and will be pink and tender inside.
For a different flavour, insert fresh mint leaves, sprigs of
fresh thyme or slivers of garlic between the chops before
barbecuing.
To serve, carve into chops.

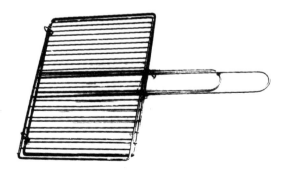

Lamb Chops Vermouth

SERVES: 4

8 lamb rib chops
Marinade:
1 cup dry vermouth
1 cup salad oil
1 tablespoon lemon juice
1 onion, chopped
2 cloves garlic, crushed
1 teaspoon dried tarragon
1 teaspoon dried basil
1 teaspoon salt
10 peppercorns, crushed

Place lamb chops in a shallow dish and pour marinade over. Cover and stand for at least 4 hours, turn chops occasionally.
Barbecue chops over medium hot coals for approximately 10-15 minutes. Baste with the marinade while cooking. Serve when chops are tender and evenly brown.
Marinade: Combine all ingredients and mix together thoroughly.

Steak Combination Kebabs
Barbecued Fillet of Steak
Barbecued Loin of Lamb

Glazed Shoulder of Lamb

SERVES: 6-8

1 x 4 lb shoulder of lamb, boned, rolled and tied
1 teaspoon salt
$\frac{1}{4}$ teaspoon pepper
Glaze:
1 cup puréed apricots
$\frac{1}{4}$ cup apple jelly
2 tablespoons finely chopped mint

Insert spit rod through centre of meat and secure. Rub with salt and pepper.
Place over medium hot coals. Cook for approximately 2-2$\frac{1}{2}$ hours or until tender. After meat has cooked for 1 hour, baste with glaze every 20 minutes.
Heat any remaining glaze and serve with the meat.
Glaze: Combine all ingredients and mix together thoroughly.

Chilli Con Carne

Barbecued Lamb

SERVES: 6-8

1 x 6 lb leg of lamb, boned
Marinade:
1 cup olive oil
$\frac{1}{4}$ cup wine vinegar
1 small onion, chopped
2 cloves garlic, crushed
freshly ground black pepper
1 teaspoon salt
sprig of rosemary

Beat lamb with a meat mallet to flatten. Place in a shallow
dish and pour over marinade. Cover and stand for several
hours, turn occasionally.
Drain and barbecue meat over medium hot coals for
approximately 2 hours or until meat is tender, turn
frequently and baste with Barbecue Sauce (see page 95)
while cooking.
To serve, carve into thick slices.
Marinade: Combine all ingredients and mix together
thoroughly.

Roast Lamb and Pineapple Stuffing

SERVES: 6-8

1 x 4 lb leg of lamb, boned
salt and pepper
Stuffing:
1 x 15 oz can crushed pineapple
1 cup soft white breadcrumbs
$\frac{1}{2}$ oz butter, melted
1 tablespoon finely chopped parsley
$\frac{1}{2}$ teaspoon dried thyme
$\frac{1}{2}$ teaspoon dried marjoram
3 tablespoons milk
1 small onion, peeled, parboiled and chopped

Season meat with salt and pepper. Place stuffing on meat, roll up and tie securely with fine string.
Insert spit rod lengthways through centre of meat and secure.
Place over medium hot coals. Cook for approximately 2-2$\frac{1}{2}$ hours or until meat is tender. While cooking, baste with reserved pineapple juice.
Stuffing: Drain and reserve syrup from pineapple.
Combine all ingredients and mix together thoroughly.

Indian Spiced Mutton

SERVES: 6

2 lb finely minced mutton
½ cup dry breadcrumbs
1 egg
salt and pepper
2 teaspoons garam marsala
12 prunes, pitted

Place all ingredients except prunes in a mixing bowl. Mix together thoroughly and shape into 12 croquettes or rissoles, placing a prune in the centre of each.
Barbecue over hot coals for approximately 10-15 minutes or until cooked.
If desired, baste with favourite marinade while cooking.

Barbecued Liver and Bacon

SERVES: 4-6

1 lamb's liver
4-6 rashers bacon, derinded
Marinade:
$\frac{1}{3}$ cup olive oil
juice of 1 lemon
salt
freshly ground pepper
1 tablespoon finely chopped parsley

Soak liver in water for 1 hour. Remove skin and cut out tubes. Cut into $\frac{1}{2}$-inch slices, with knife in a slanting position. Place liver in a shallow dish, pour over marinade, cover and stand for 1 hour.
Drain liver and barbecue over medium hot coals for approximately 10-12 minutes.
Grill bacon until crisp and brown.
Heat remaining marinade and serve with liver and bacon.
Marinade: Combine all ingredients and mix together thoroughly.

Barbecued Steaks

Rather than cutting steaks into individual portions and cooking these separately, try cooking steaks in large slices and then cutting the cooked steaks into serving portions. Steak should be well trimmed and all excess fat removed. Barbecue rump steak (or sirloin steak) over medium coals for approximately 45 minutes-1 hour, according to taste. Cook boned sirloin steak (or boned rib steak) over slow coals for approximately $1\frac{1}{2}$-2 hours, according to taste. Cook fillet steak (or tenderloin steak) over medium coals for 30-45 minutes, according to taste.

When individual steaks are barbecued, cook over medium hot coals for approximately 10-20 minutes, depending on whether steak is to be served rare, medium or well done. It is important to remember to turn the steak frequently while cooking so that the juices are retained inside the meat. Should you leave the meat without turning for some time, you will notice a quantity of blood on top, whereas by turning the meat frequently, the juices run up and down inside the meat and it will remain moist.

The steak may be smeared with pâté, horseradish relish or mustard to add flavour while cooking.

To serve, carve steak and either place on dinner plates or for a buffet dinner party, serve on slices of French bread.

Barbecued Sirloin Steaks

6 x 8 oz sirloin steaks (or rib steaks)
Sauce:
1 x 13 fl oz can beer
1 tablespoon chilli sauce
¼ cup salad oil
2 tablespoons soy sauce
1 tablespoon French mustard
½ teaspoon Tabasco sauce
1 onion, chopped
2 cloves garlic, crushed
salt and pepper

Brush meat with sauce.
Barbecue over medium hot coals for 10-20 minutes,
according to taste. Baste occasionally with the sauce while
cooking.
Heat the remaining sauce and serve with the steak.
Sauce: Combine all ingredients and mix together
thoroughly.

Ginger Steak

6 pieces porterhouse steak
1 oz butter, melted
Marinade:
$\frac{1}{4}$ **cup soy sauce**
$\frac{1}{2}$ **cup pineapple juice**
1 tablespoon ground ginger
2 tablespoons dry sherry
$\frac{1}{2}$ **teaspoon dry mustard**
1 clove garlic, crushed

Place steak in a large shallow dish. Pour marinade over, cover and stand for at least 4 hours.
Drain meat and barbecue over medium hot coals for 10-20 minutes, according to taste. Baste occasionally with melted butter while cooking.
Heat remaining marinade and pour over steak before serving.
Marinade: Combine all ingredients and mix together thoroughly.

Grilled Steak and Wine Sauce

SERVES: 4-6

4-6 T-bone or porterhouse steaks
1 tablespoon finely chopped onion
1 oz butter or margarine
1 tablespoon ($\frac{1}{2}$ oz) plain flour
$\frac{1}{4}$ cup water
$\frac{3}{4}$ cup claret
salt and pepper
$\frac{1}{4}$ cup chopped parsley

Barbecue steaks over medium hot coals for 10-20 minutes, according to taste. In the meantime, cook onion in butter until golden brown. Mix flour and water until smooth, add to the onion mixture, add the claret. Bring to the boil, stirring continuously. Season to taste with salt and pepper and simmer for 10 minutes. Add the parsley and serve immediately with the grilled steaks.

Quick Garlic Steaks

SERVES: 6-8

6-8 pieces fillet steak, 1-inch thick (or tenderloin steak)
2 oz butter or margarine, melted
1 clove garlic, crushed
juice of 2 lemons
2 tablespoons Worcestershire sauce
salt
freshly ground pepper

Cut steaks almost through the centre and open out. Beat steaks with a meat mallet until $\frac{1}{4}$-inch thick. Combine melted butter and garlic, dip steaks in butter to coat.
Barbecue steaks over medium hot coals for 5-15 minutes, according to taste. Baste while cooking with garlic butter. Add lemon juice, Worcestershire sauce and salt and pepper to remaining garlic butter, mix well and pour over steaks before serving.

Steak with Blue Cheese

SERVES: 4

4 pieces rump steak (or sirloin steak)
2 oz butter, softened
2 oz blue vein cheese
2 tablespoons finely chopped parsley
freshly ground pepper
extra 1 oz butter, melted
1 teaspoon Worcestershire sauce

Make a slit in each steak, parallel to the surface of the meat.
Cream softened butter with blue vein cheese and parsley,
place inside pocket of each steak. Sprinkle steaks with
pepper. Mix extra butter and Worcestershire sauce together.
Barbecue steaks over medium hot coals for 10-20 minutes,
according to taste. Baste with the butter mixture
occasionally while cooking.

Chilli Con Carne

SERVES: 4-6

1 onion, chopped
2 cloves garlic, crushed
1 tablespoon oil
1 lb minced steak
1 x 15 oz can condensed tomato soup
1 teaspoon salt
1 tablespoon chilli powder
$\frac{1}{2}$ cup water
1 green pepper, seeded and chopped
2 cups cooked red kidney beans or 2 x 10 oz cans
kidney beans, drained

Sauté onion and garlic in hot oil in a large heavy based
frying pan. Add minced beef and cook until meat browns,
stir continuously. Add soup, salt, chilli powder and water.
Cover and simmer for 10 minutes, stir occasionally.
Add green pepper and beans, simmer for a further 20
minutes and serve hot.
Serve with boiled rice.

Veal Cutlets

For each serving:

2 veal cutlets (or veal rib chops)
4 mushrooms
2 tablespoons white wine
2 tablespoons cream
salt and pepper
1 tablespoon finely chopped chives

Place cutlets side by side in centre of a large piece of greased, doubled aluminium foil. Peel and slice mushrooms thinly, place on top of cutlets. Turn up sides of foil. Add wine, cream, salt and pepper and chives. Seal foil securely. Place packages on barbecue over medium hot coals and cook for approximately 30 minutes or until meat is tender. Turn once while cooking.

Veal Chops

For each serving:

1 veal loin chop
1 tomato, skinned and chopped
$\frac{1}{2}$ tablespoon finely chopped onion
$\frac{1}{2}$ tablespoon finely chopped chives
pinch of dried tarragon
pinch of dried marjoram
2 tablespoons finely chopped cucumber with peel
salt and pepper
1 tablespoon oil
1 tablespoon sherry

Place chop on large piece of doubled aluminium foil. Add remaining ingredients, turning sides of foil up before adding the oil and sherry. Seal foil securely.
Place packages on barbecue over medium hot coals and cook for approximately 30 minutes or until meat is tender. Turn once while cooking.

Whole Loin of Pork

Ask butcher to cut through bone only, so that chops can be cut with a knife when cooked. Rub salt into skin of pork to make good crackling. Slivers of garlic may be inserted between the chops if desired.
Barbecue over medium coals for approximately 45 minutes-1 hour or until meat is tender. Barbecue on the bone side mainly and cut down cooking time on the skin side.
Watch pork carefully while barbecuing so that the crackling does not catch and burn.
To serve carve, into individual chops.

Peppered Pork

SERVES: 6

6 thin pork loin chops
1 oz butter, melted
1 teaspoon salt
1 tablespoon black peppercorns, crushed
$\frac{1}{4}$ cup blackcurrant jelly
12 canned peach halves

Brush the chops with melted butter and sprinkle with salt. Press the crushed peppercorns evenly into the chops. Barbecue over medium coals for approximately 15-20 minutes. Place a spoonful of blackcurrant jelly in each peach half and place on side of barbecue to warm through. When pork chops are tender and evenly brown, serve with the warmed peach halves.

Pork and Apple

For each serving:

1 pork leg chop (or fresh ham centre slice)
$\frac{1}{2}$ **cooking apple**
salt and pepper
$\frac{1}{4}$ **tablespoon finely chopped fresh sage**
**2 tablespoons cider or 1 tablespoon cider and 1
    tablespoon cream**

Remove excess fat from chop. Place on large piece of
greased, doubled aluminium foil. Peel, core and thinly slice
the apple and place over chop. Sprinkle with seasonings.
Turn sides of foil up and add cider. Seal foil securely.
Cook on barbecue over hot coals for approximately 1-1$\frac{1}{4}$
hours or until meat is tender.

Barbecued Spareribs

SERVES: 4

1 clove garlic, crushed
salt and pepper
pinch of monosodium glutamate
1 tablespoon ($\frac{1}{2}$ oz) brown sugar
1 teaspoon paprika pepper
1 teaspoon dry mustard
8-10 pork spareribs
commercial barbecue sauce

Combine garlic, salt and pepper, monosodium glutamate, sugar, paprika pepper and mustard and rub spareribs with the seasoning.
Barbecue over medium coals, turning frequently and basting with the barbecue sauce while cooking. Cook for approximately 15-20 minutes or until spareribs are tender.

Ham and Pineapple

SERVES: 6

6 slices cooked ham, $\frac{1}{2}$-inch thick
6 slices fresh or canned pineapple
Glaze:
$\frac{1}{2}$ cup honey
$\frac{1}{4}$ cup lemon juice
$\frac{1}{2}$ teaspoon ground cloves
2 teaspoons soy sauce

Barbecue ham and pineapple quickly over hot coals, basting frequently with the glaze.
Serve when warmed through and lightly brown.
Glaze: Combine all ingredients and mix together thoroughly.

Minted Lamb Kebabs with Rice Pilaf

Kebabs

A meal on a stick! Steak, veal, lamb, pork, poultry and seafood, all are suitable for kebabs. The combination of ingredients is innumerable and you can make up your own variations to suit family and friends.

Cheaper cuts of meat can be utilized. By cutting meat into bite size pieces and placing in a marinade for several hours before barbecuing, coarser grained meats become tender and tasty. Baste kebabs with melted butter, oil, your favourite sauce or any remaining marinade. Remember to cut firmer ingredients into smaller pieces than the softer ones. For example, buy small cherry tomatoes and use them whole, but cut onions and peppers into pieces so that all ingredients will be cooked at the same time. In fact, some people like to parboil onions and peppers before barbecuing.

For a main course, make long kebabs on stainless steel skewers and serve on a bed of boiled rice or pilaf. For an appetizer, make smaller kebabs on bamboo skewers and serve directly from the grill.

For an informal barbecue party, prepare ingredients and place in large colourful bowls, ask guests to make up their own kebabs. Serve with crisp salads, pickles and relishes. Hot crusty bread is also a good accompaniment.

Chicken and Orange Kebabs

SERVES: 4

3 oranges
3-6 rashers bacon
1 lb cooked chicken
24 small mushroom caps, peeled
2 oz butter or margarine
Basting sauce:
juice of 1 large orange
extra 2 oz butter or margarine, melted

Peel oranges, remove pith and divide into segments.
Remove rind from bacon, fry gently and cut into 1-inch
pieces. Remove skin from chicken and cut into 1-inch
cubes. Sauté mushroom caps lightly in butter.
Alternate orange segments, bacon, chicken and mushroom
caps onto skewers.
Barbecue kebabs over hot coals, turn and baste frequently
with the sauce while cooking.
Serve when kebabs are warmed through and lightly
browned on all sides.
Basting sauce: Mix orange juice and melted butter
together.

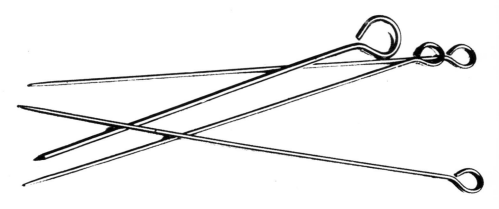

Armenian Shish Kebabs

SERVES: 6

2 lb lean lamb, cut into 1½-inch cubes
1 green pepper, seeded
1 red pepper, seeded
12 small white onions, halved
Marinade:
½ cup salad oil
¼ cup lemon juice
1 teaspoon salt
½ teaspoon dried marjoram
½ teaspoon dried thyme
freshly ground pepper
1 clove garlic, crushed
½ cup chopped onion
2 tablespoons chopped parsley

Place meat in a mixing bowl and pour over the marinade.
Mix well, cover and stand for at least 3-4 hours.
Cut peppers into 1½-inch pieces. Drain meat and place on
skewers alternating with pieces of pepper and halved
onions.
Barbecue over hot coals for approximately 20 minutes or
until meat is tender. Turn kebabs frequently and baste with
the marinade while cooking.
Marinade: Combine all ingredients and mix together
thoroughly.

Minted Lamb Kebabs

SERVES: 4

2 lb lean lamb, cut into 1½-inch cubes
8 small tomatoes
12 small mushrooms
Marinade:
2 tablespoons chopped fresh mint
½ cup vinegar
2½ tablespoons (1 oz) brown sugar
pinch of dry mustard
½ teaspoon salt
2 oz butter
1 teaspoon grated lemon rind
¼ cup white wine

Place meat in a bowl, add marinade and mix well. Cover and stand for 1-2 hours.
Drain meat and alternate meat, tomatoes and mushrooms onto skewers.
Barbecue over hot coals for approximately 20 minutes, turning and basting frequently with marinade while cooking.
Marinade: Place all ingredients except white wine in saucepan. Bring to the boil, take off heat and allow to stand for 30 minutes, add white wine.

Lamb Kidney Kebabs

Allow 3 kidneys and 3 bacon rashers for each person.
Wash and skin kidneys, cut in halves and remove cores. Cut rind from bacon and cut each rasher in half. Wrap each piece around a piece of kidney, place on skewers.
Barbecue over hot coals for approximately 15-20 minutes or until kidneys are cooked and bacon is crisp and brown. Turn kebabs frequently while cooking.
Variations: Replace kidney with pieces of lamb's fry, cooked brain or sweetbread.

Mexican Steak Kebabs

SERVES: 4-5

1$\frac{1}{2}$ lb round steak, cut into 1$\frac{1}{2}$-inch cubes
Mexican sauce:
$\frac{1}{2}$ cup chopped onion
1 tablespoon olive oil
1 cup red wine vinegar
$\frac{1}{2}$ teaspoon salt
$\frac{1}{2}$ teaspoon dried oregano
$\frac{1}{2}$ teaspoon dried cumin
$\frac{1}{2}$ teaspoon ground cloves
$\frac{1}{2}$ teaspoon ground cinnamon
$\frac{1}{2}$ teaspoon pepper
1 clove garlic, crushed

Place meat on skewers.
Baste with sauce and barbecue over hot coals for
approximately 12-15 minutes or until meat is tender. Turn
frequently and baste with the sauce while cooking.
Mexican sauce: Combine all ingredients and mix together
thoroughly.

Steak Combination Kebabs

SERVES: 4

1½ lb lean rump steak (or sirloin steak)
12 small onions
2 green peppers
12 small tomatoes
2 oz butter, melted

Cut steak into 1½-inch cubes.
Parboil onions. Seed peppers and cut into 1½-inch pieces.
Alternate steak, onions, pieces of pepper and tomatoes onto skewers. Baste with melted butter.
Barbecue over hot coals for approximately 12-15 minutes or until meat is tender. Turn kebabs frequently and baste with melted butter again before serving.

Steak and Pineapple Kebabs

SERVES: 4-6

1½ lb lean rump steak (or sirloin steak), cut into
   1-inch cubes
8 oz button mushrooms
1 green pepper, seeded
1 x 15 oz can pineapple pieces or chunks of fresh
   pineapple
Marinade:
2 cups tomato juice
½ cup vinegar
2 tablespoons French mustard
1 tablespoon (½ oz) sugar
2 teaspoons salt
freshly ground pepper

Place steak in a mixing bowl, pour over marinade. Mix
well, cover and stand for 2 hours.
Peel mushrooms and remove stalks. Cut pepper into 1-inch
pieces. Drain pineapple pieces. Drain meat and alternate
meat, mushrooms, pepper and pineapple pieces onto
skewers.
Barbecue over hot coals, turning and basting frequently
with marinade while cooking. Cook for approximately 12-15
minutes or until meat is tender.
Marinade: Combine all ingredients and mix together
thoroughly.

Steak and Crayfish Kebabs

SERVES: 6-8

1 large green crayfish (or lobster)
2 green peppers
1½ lb lean rump steak (or sirloin steak), cut into
   1½-inch cubes
Sauce:
¼ cup sauterne
¼ cup lemon juice
¼ cup salad oil

Remove meat from tail of crayfish, cut into 1½-inch chunks.
Seed peppers and cut into 1½-inch pieces. Alternate steak,
crayfish and pieces of pepper onto skewers.
Barbecue over hot coals for approximately 12-15 minutes
or until meat and crayfish is tender. Turn frequently and
baste with sauce while cooking.
Sauce: Combine all ingredients and mix together thoroughly.

Veal Kebabs in Chinese Marinade

SERVES: 6

2 lb boneless leg veal, cut into 1-inch pieces
Marinade:
½ cup soy sauce
¼ cup salad oil
1 teaspoon ground ginger
1 teaspoon dry mustard
1 teaspoon sugar
3 cloves garlic, crushed

Place meat in a mixing bowl, pour over marinade, cover and stand for 2-3 hours. Drain meat and thread onto skewers.
Barbecue over hot coals for approximately 20 minutes or until meat is tender. Turn and baste frequently with the marinade while cooking.
Marinade: Combine all ingredients and mix together thoroughly.

Pork and Apricot Kebabs

SERVES: 6-8

2 lb boneless shoulder pork
8 oz dried apricots
marsala
Marinade:
1 cup pineapple juice
$\frac{1}{2}$ cup soy sauce
1 clove garlic, crushed
2 teaspoons chopped preserved ginger

Cut pork into $1\frac{1}{2}$-inch cubes and place in a mixing bowl,
pour over marinade, mix well and cover. Stand for 1 hour.
Drain meat and apricots and place alternately on skewers.
Barbecue over hot coals for approximately 20-25 minutes or
until meat is tender. Turn frequently and baste with the
marinade while cooking.
Place dried apricots in another bowl, cover with marsala
and stand for 1 hour.
Marinade: Combine all ingredients and mix together
thoroughly.
Variation: Replace pork with pieces of lamb.

Polynesian Pork Kebabs

SERVES: 4

1½ lb boneless leg pork
Marinade:
1 finely chopped onion
1-2 cloves garlic, crushed
4 Brazil nuts, grated
¼ cup lemon juice
¼ cup soy sauce
1 teaspoon pepper
few drops Tabasco sauce
1 teaspoon ground coriander
2 tablespoons (1 oz) brown sugar
2 tablespoons salad oil

Cut pork into 1-inch cubes. Place meat in a mixing bowl, pour over marinade, mix well, cover and stand for at least 2 hours. Drain meat and place on skewers.
Barbecue over hot coals for approximately 20-25 minutes or until meat is tender. While cooking, baste frequently with marinade and turn regularly.
Heat any remaining marinade and serve with the kebabs.
Marinade: Combine all ingredients and mix together thoroughly.

Satay

1 lb cooked meat
Marinade:
1 teaspoon soy sauce
1 teaspoon Tabasco sauce
1 tablespoon white vinegar
2 tablespoons salad oil
1 tablespoon ($\frac{1}{2}$ oz) brown sugar
1 clove garlic, crushed

Cut meat into $\frac{1}{2}$-inch cubes. Place in a mixing bowl, pour over marinade and mix thoroughly, cover and stand for 3-4 hours.
Place meat on fine skewers and barbecue over hot coals for approximately 5 minutes or until meat is just heated through, turn frequently.
Marinade: Combine all ingredients and mix thoroughly.

Vegetable Kebabs

Spear a selection of vegetables onto skewers and serve with grilled steak, chops or sausages. Try small tomatoes, mushroom caps, chunks of fresh pineapple, parboiled corncobs (cut into 1-inch rings) and small parboiled onions. Barbecue over medium coals, turning frequently and basting with melted butter or margarine while cooking.

Barbecued Burgers

Hamburgers are a delicious favourite with young and old. Seasoned with salt and pepper and barbecued directly over glowing coals or on a skillet or hotplate, nothing could be more tasty. They are ideal for a large group of friends as they can be prepared in advance and guests can add their own accompaniments depending on their individual tastes.

Buy freshly minced steak or ask your butcher to mince your favourite cut of steak specially for you. If the steak is particularly lean, add some shredded suet to the meat mixture before shaping the hamburgers, they will be moist and tender when cooked. Roll the prepared mince out to the desired thickness and cut into rounds a little larger than the bread rolls to be filled. The hamburgers will shrink slightly while cooking. For a smaller number of people you may like to serve thicker hamburgers shaped individually. Place a layer on a tray, cover with clear plastic wrap or aluminium foil and place another layer on top. Place in refrigerator until ready to cook.

Barbecued hamburgers should be juicy and tender when cooked, serve between thick slices of fresh bread or toast or serve in hamburger rolls. Bread and rolls may be spread with butter or mayonnaise. Add a fried egg or grilled bacon for extra nourishment for children. Serve relishes, mustards, pickles and salad ingredients in separate bowls and ask guests to help themselves.

Grilled Hamburgers

SERVES: 6

1½ lb finely minced steak
1 onion, finely chopped
1 teaspoon salt
freshly ground pepper
6 hamburgers rolls, split, toasted and buttered
Barbecue sauce:
1 cup tomato ketchup
2 teaspoons Worcestershire sauce
½ teaspoon celery salt
few drops chilli sauce

Combine minced steak, onion and seasonings in a mixing
bowl, mix together thoroughly. Shape into 6 hamburgers,
approximately ½-inch thick.
Barbecue over hot coals for approximately 8-10 minutes on
each side or until cooked. Baste hamburgers with the
barbecue sauce while cooking.
Place in the prepared rolls and serve any remaining
barbecue sauce with the hamburgers.
Barbecue sauce: Combine all ingredients and mix
together thoroughly.

Hawaiian Hamburgers

SERVES: 8

2 lb finely minced steak
1 egg
1 onion, finely chopped
½ cup dry breadcrumbs
2 tablespoons tomato sauce
2 tablespoons (1 oz) brown sugar
1 teaspoon French mustard
1 teaspoon salt
commercial barbecue sauce
8 slices fresh or canned pineapple

Combine minced steak, egg, onion, breadcrumbs, tomato sauce, sugar, mustard and seasonings in a mixing bowl. Mix together thoroughly and shape into 8 hamburgers. Barbecue over hot coals for approximately 8-10 minutes on each side or until cooked. While cooking, brush occasionally with barbecue sauce.
Barbecue slices of pineapple until golden brown, top each hamburger with a slice and serve immediately.

Pizza Burgers

SERVES: 6

1½ lb finely minced steak
⅓ cup grated Parmesan cheese
¼ cup finely chopped onion
¼ cup chopped green olives
1 teaspoon salt
freshly ground pepper
1 teaspoon dried oregano
1 x 5 oz can tomato paste
6 slices mozzarella cheese
6 slices tomato
6 hamburger rolls, split, toasted and spread with
   mayonnaise

Combine minced steak, Parmesan cheese, onion, olives,
seasonings and tomato paste in a mixing bowl, mix
together thoroughly.
Shape into 8 hamburgers and barbecue over hot coals for
approximately 10 minutes, turn. Top each hamburger with
a slice of mozzarella cheese and tomato. Barbecue for a
further 5 minutes or until hamburgers are cooked.
Serve in prepared rolls.

Glazed Frankfurter

Surprise Hamburgers

SERVES: 8

2 lb finely minced steak
2 eggs
$\frac{1}{2}$ cup soft white breadcrumbs
1 teaspoon salt
freshly ground pepper
8 hamburger rolls, buttered
Fillings:
8 slices processed Cheddar cheese, spread with
   mustard or fruit chutney.
8 thin slices onion, spread with chilli sauce.
8 slices tomato, spread with mayonnaise and
   sprinkled with chopped chives.
8 slices ham, spread with French mustard.
Sliced dill pickles.
Horseradish relish.

Combine minced steak, eggs, breadcrumbs and seasonings
in a mixing bowl. Mix together thoroughly and shape into
16 thin patties. Place chosen filling on 8 of the patties,
top with remaining patties and press edges together firmly.
Barbecue over hot coals for approximately 8-10 minutes on
each side or until cooked.
Serve in buttered rolls.

Wine Hamburgers

SERVES: 8

2 lb finely minced steak
1 cup soft white breadcrumbs
1 egg
$\frac{1}{4}$ cup Burgundy
1 onion, finely chopped
1 teaspoon salt
freshly ground pepper
8 thick slices French bread, cut diagonally and
    buttered
Burgundy sauce:
2 oz butter or margarine
1 large onion, finely chopped
$\frac{1}{4}$ cup Burgundy

Combine minced steak, breadcrumbs, egg, Burgundy, onion
and seasonings in a mixing bowl. Mix together thoroughly
and shape into 8 hamburgers, approximately 1-inch thick.
Brush with the sauce and barbecue over hot coals for
approximately 8-10 minutes on each side or until cooked,
brush occasionally with the sauce while cooking.
Serve on the buttered French bread.
Burgundy sauce: Melt butter in a saucepan, add onion
and cook until golden and transparent, add Burgundy and
simmer for 5 minutes.

Sausages and Frankfurters

There are innumerable types of sausages and frankfurters available. Adapt any of the following recipes using your favourite type.

Sausages and frankfurters are firm favourites with children and teenagers and they are an economical meal for a large number of guests. They can be included in casseroles which can be prepared in advance in the kitchen or they can be cooked directly on the barbecue grill. Sausages may be parboiled before barbecuing, perhaps a little flavour is lost but there is less likelihood of sausages being raw inside or bursting while cooking. If sausages are barbecued raw, cook over medium coals, turning frequently until they are cooked through and evenly brown outside.

Apricot Glazed Sausages

SERVES: 6

2 lb thick beef or pork sausages
Apricot sauce:
2 tablespoons salad oil
2 tablespoons vinegar
$\frac{1}{2}$ cup apricot nectar
$\frac{1}{2}$ cup tomato sauce
1 tablespoon ($\frac{1}{2}$ oz) brown sugar
2 tablespoons grated onion
$\frac{1}{2}$ teaspoon Worcestershire sauce
1 teaspoon salt
$\frac{1}{2}$ teaspoon dried oregano
few drops Tabasco sauce

Barbecue sausages over medium coals, turning frequently
and basting with the sauce while cooking.
Barbecue sausages for approximately 15 minutes or until
cooked and golden brown.
Reheat remaining sauce and serve with the sausages.
Apricot sauce: Place all ingredients in a heavy based
saucepan. Bring to the boil, stirring occasionally. Cover
and simmer gently for 10 minutes.
Note: This sauce keeps well for 1-2 weeks in a sealed
container in the refrigerator.

Barbecued Bratwurst Sausages

SERVES: 4-5

1 lb bratwurst sausages
2 x 13 fl oz cans beer
1 onion, thinly sliced
1 teaspoon Worcestershire sauce

Place all ingredients in a heavy based saucepan or flameproof casserole. Bring to simmering point and simmer gently for approximately 5 minutes, drain.
Barbecue sausages, turning frequently, for approximately 10 minutes or until evenly brown.

Barbecued Polish Sausages

SERVES: 4-5

1½ cups hot water
1½ cups red wine
1 lb Polish sausages
German mustard
8-10 slices rye bread

Pour water and red wine into a heavy based saucepan or flameproof casserole, bring to the boil. Add sausages and simmer gently for approximately 5-10 minutes. Drain and cool sausages.
Place on barbecue and turning frequently, cook for 15-20 minutes until evenly brown.
Serve with mustard and rye bread.

54

Heidelberg Dinner

SERVES: 8-10

4 cooking apples
1 small red cabbage, coarsely shredded
$\frac{1}{2}$ cup apple cider
$\frac{1}{4}$ cup salad oil
2 tablespoons red wine vinegar
2 tablespoons (1 oz) brown sugar
2 bay leaves
$\frac{1}{2}$ teaspoon salt
freshly ground pepper
1 lb Polish sausages
1 lb bratwurst sausages

Core apples, do not peel. Cut apple into thin slices.
Combine all ingredients except sausages in a heavy based
saucepan or flameproof casserole, mix together thoroughly.
Cover and place on barbecue over medium hot coals for
approximately 1 hour or until cabbage is tender, stir
occasionally while cooking.
Barbecue sausages, turning frequently, cook for
approximately 15-20 minutes or until sausages are evenly
brown and cooked through.
Serve sausages with the red cabbage casserole.

Sausages with Bacon and Cheese

SERVES: 3-4

1 lb thick pork sausages
4 oz Cheddar cheese, sliced
6 rashers bacon, derinded
3 tablespoons fruit chutney

Barbecue sausages over medium coals for approximately 15 minutes. Slit sausages lengthways, almost through. Place slices of cheese in the sausages and press together again. Spread bacon rashers with the chutney and wrap around the sausages, secure ends with cocktail sticks. Place on barbecue again and turning frequently, cook until cheese begins to melt and bacon is crisp and golden brown. Remove cocktail sticks before serving.

Sausages Supreme

Place thick pork sausages in a heavy based saucepan, cover with cold water and bring to the boil, simmer for 5-10 minutes. Drain and cool.
Place sausages on barbecue over medium coals and turning frequently, cook until evenly brown.
When ready to serve sausages, slit lengthways, not quite through, and place 2-3 cold oysters inside each. Serve immediately.

Frankfurter and Pineapple Kebabs

Cut each frankfurter into 4 pieces. Alternate on skewers with pieces of canned or fresh pineapple. Brush with melted butter or margarine.

Barbecue over medium coals for 7-10 minutes or until golden brown. Turn frequently while cooking and baste with melted butter.

Toast split frankfurter rolls over coals and spread with butter.

Serve kebabs in bread rolls with mustard if desired.

Frankfurters wrapped in Bacon

Slit frankfurters lengthways, not quite through and to within $\frac{1}{4}$-inch of each end. Spread inside generously with favourite pickle or relish and wrap a derinded rasher of bacon around each frankfurter, securing the ends with cocktail sticks.

Barbecue over medium coals until frankfurters are hot and bacon is crisp and brown. Remove cocktail sticks before serving.

Glazed Frankfurters

SERVES: 8-10

2 lb frankfurters
Sauce:
1 cup canned apricots, drained and puréed
½ cup tomato sauce
⅓ cup vinegar
¼ cup sherry
2 tablespoons soy sauce
2 tablespoons honey
¼ teaspoon ground ginger
¼ teaspoon salt
freshly ground pepper

Barbecue frankfurters over medium coals for approximately 7-10 minutes, turning and basting frequently with the sauce while cooking.
Serve frankfurters when hot and glazed. Heat remaining sauce in a heavy based saucepan and serve separately.
Sauce: Combine all ingredients and mix together thoroughly.

Italian Style Frankfurters

SERVES: 4-5

8 oz minced steak
½ cup chopped onion
½ cup chopped celery
2 oz butter or margarine
½ cup tomato ketchup
½ cup water
1 beef stock cube
2 tablespoons German mustard
salt and pepper
1 lb frankfurters

Brown minced steak, onion and celery in butter in a heavy
based saucepan or flameproof casserole. Add tomato
ketchup, water, beef stock cube and mustard, mix together
thoroughly and simmer uncovered for 15-20 minutes.
Season to taste with salt and pepper.
Slit frankfurters lengthways, but not quite through.
Barbecue over medium coals for 7-10 minutes, turn
frequently while cooking.
When heated through, serve with the meat sauce spooned
over them.

Barbecued Poultry

Chicken can be cooked on a barbecue in a number of ways. It can be cooked whole on a rotisserie or halved or cut into portions and grilled over glowing coals. For easy eating, when catering for a large number of people, bone chickens when raw and after cooking, cut into bite size pieces and hand around on large serving plates. Chicken, cut into pieces, placed on skewers and barbecued, makes delicious kebabs, baste while cooking with your favourite sauce. When cooking chicken pieces, cook them longer on the bone side than the meat side. This protects the meat from becoming charred while cooking, it will remain moist and tender and will be golden brown when cooked. Baste the pieces of chicken before cooking with melted butter or oil and again when cooking is completed.

Barbecued Chicken Halves

SERVES: 4

4 chicken halves
Marinade:
1 cup sherry or apple juice
½ cup salad oil
1 onion, finely chopped
1 tablespoon French mustard
1 tablespoon mixed dried herbs
1 teaspoon salt
freshly ground pepper
1 tablespoon Worcestershire sauce
1 teaspoon soy sauce

Place chicken halves in a shallow dish, pour marinade over.
Cover and stand for several hours, turn meat occasionally.
Drain chicken and reserve marinade.
Barbecue chicken over medium hot coals for approximately
25-35 minutes or until tender. Allow more cooking time
on the bone side than the flesh side. Baste with the
marinade while cooking.
Marinade: Combine all ingredients and mix together
thoroughly.

Barbecued Drumsticks

12 chicken drumsticks
Marinade:
$\frac{1}{4}$ **cup tomato ketchup**
2-3 tablespoons lemon juice
2 tablespoons soy sauce
$\frac{1}{4}$ **cup salad oil**
$\frac{1}{2}$ **teaspoon monosodium glutamate**

Place drumsticks in a shallow dish, add marinade. Cover
and stand for at least 2 hours, turn drumsticks occasionally.
Drain meat and reserve marinade.
Barbecue drumsticks over medium hot coals for
approximately 20-25 minutes or until tender. Baste
occasionally with the marinade while cooking.
Marinade: Combine all ingredients and mix together
thoroughly.

Chicken on the Spit

SERVES: 4

1 x 3 lb chicken
2 teaspoons salt
freshly ground pepper
2-4 oz butter or margarine, melted

Wash and dry chicken, sprinkle salt and pepper in cavity.
Truss chicken firmly and insert spit rod through centre of
bird from neck to tail. Make sure chicken is held firmly in
place and will not work loose while cooking.
Cook over medium hot coals for approximately $1\frac{1}{4}$-$1\frac{3}{4}$ hours
or until tender. When cooked, drumsticks should feel soft
and move easily. Baste chicken frequently with butter while
cooking.
Cut chicken into 4 portions to serve.
Note: While cooking, chicken may be basted with favourite
sauce or marinade instead of butter.

Golden Chicken

SERVES: 4

1 x $3\frac{1}{2}$ lb chicken
2 tablespoons curry powder
1 teaspoon salt
$\frac{1}{2}$ cup honey
2 tablespoons French mustard

Cut chicken into serving pieces. Combine curry powder and
salt and sprinkle over chicken pieces. Mix honey and
mustard together.
Barbecue chicken over medium hot coals for approximately
20-25 minutes or until tender, baste frequently with the
honey mixture while cooking. Allow more cooking time on
the bone side than the flesh side.

Chicken Teriyaki

SERVES: 4

1 x 3½ lb chicken
Marinade:
½ cup soy sauce
¼ cup honey
½ teaspoon monosodium glutamate
1 clove garlic, crushed
½ teaspoon ground ginger

Cut chicken into serving pieces and place in a shallow
dish. Pour marinade over, cover and chill for at least 8
hours, turn meat occasionally. Drain chicken and reserve
marinade.
Barbecue chicken pieces over medium hot coals for
approximately 20-25 minutes or until tender. Allow more
cooking time on the bone side than the flesh side. Baste
with the marinade while cooking.
Marinade: Combine all ingredients and mix together
thoroughly.

Basting Barbecued Chicken Halves

Devilled Chicken

2 x 2½ lb chickens
Sauce:
2 oz butter or margarine
½ cup finely chopped onion
1½ cups tomato juice
⅓ cup lemon juice
1 tablespoon Worcestershire sauce
1 tablespoon paprika
1 teaspoon sugar
1 teaspoon salt
freshly ground pepper

Cut chickens into serving pieces.
Barbecue over medium hot coals for approximately 20-25 minutes or until chicken is tender. Allow more cooking time on the bone side than the flesh side. Baste with the sauce while cooking.
Serve any remaining sauce with the chicken.
Sauce: Melt butter in a saucepan, add onion and saute until golden brown. Add remaining ingredients, heat until boiling. Keep warm while basting chicken pieces.

Barbecued Sucking Pig

Barbecue the Beast

Give your friends a surprise, barbecue a lamb or sucking pig when you next entertain. What a delicious flavour, they will talk about it for months. With these recipes to guide you it is so simple.

Barbecued Lamb

For barbecuing, choose a lamb 30-35 lb in weight. Allow approximately $\frac{1}{2}$-$\frac{3}{4}$ lb carcase weight for each serving. A lamb weighing 30 lb will therefore serve 40-60 people. Cook lamb approximately 20 minutes for each pound.
Split lamb in half lengthways. Make small incisions in skin of lamb approximately 3-inches apart, insert slivers of garlic and fresh thyme leaves.
The larger the lamb, the further away from the coals it should be while cooking.
The lamb can be turned easily by placing each half in a stainless steel basket which hangs from a tall tripod over the barbecue or place on grill 14-16 inches above hot coals. Turn frequently and allow more cooking time on the bone side—three times longer than the skin side. While cooking, baste with a mixture of claret and finely chopped mint leaves.
When serving Barbecued Lamb at a buffet party, cut meat into bite size pieces and arrange on large trays. If guests are seated, carve meat and place on dinner plates.

Sucking Pig

For barbecuing, a sucking pig should weigh under 20 lb. Allow approximately 1 lb carcase weight for each serving. A pig weighing 12-14 lb will therefore serve 12-14 people. Cook approximately 20-25 minutes for each pound.
The pig will be cooked more successfully and easily if cut in half. Cut pig lengthways down the centre and score the legs. Rub the skin with plenty of salt to give a crisp crackling.
The pig can be turned easily by placing each half in a stainless steel basket which hangs from a tall tripod over the barbecue or place on grill 14-16 inches above the hot coals. Turn frequently and allow more cooking time on the bone side—three times longer than the skin side. Too much cooking on the skin side will burn the skin and ruin the crackling.
When serving Sucking Pig at a buffet party, cut into bite size pieces and arrange on large trays. If guests are seated, carve the meat and place on dinner plates.

Barbecued Fish

The following recipes will appeal especially to the fishermen. Whole fish, fish steaks, fillets of fish and shellfish, all can be barbecued successfully.

Whole fish may be barbecued in wire baskets, turning frequently. No basting is required, but when cooked and ready to serve, brush the fish with butter and lemon juice and season with salt and pepper. Small fish, freshly caught, may be threaded on stainless steel skewers for barbecuing or they may be cooked in wire baskets placed flat over the fire.

Fish steaks, fillets of fish and shellfish may be barbecued directly over glowing coals or cooked in a cast iron skillet or on a hotplate. Choose which ever method you prefer. Serve the freshly barbecued fish as an appetizer or main course.

Remember fish is delicate so handle it carefully. Serve when the translucent flesh has turned opaque and flakes easily with a fork, it will be moist and tender.

Baked Stuffed Fish

SERVES: 4-6

1 x 2½-3 lb snapper (or bass)
3 rashers bacon, derinded
freshly ground pepper
Stuffing:
2 oz butter or margarine
½ cup chopped onion
½ cup chopped celery
2 tablespoons finely chopped parsley
½ teaspoon salt
½ teaspoon dried thyme
1 cup soft white breadcrumbs

Wash fish and dry thoroughly. Place stuffing in cavity of
fish, close opening with fine skewers or cocktail sticks.
Place on large piece of greased, doubled aluminium foil,
place bacon rashers over top and sprinkle with pepper.
Wrap fish securely in foil and cook over medium hot coals
for approximately 1-1¼ hours or until fish flakes easily with
a fork. Turn occasionally while cooking.
Stuffing: Melt butter and place in a bowl with remaining
ingredients. Mix together thoroughly.

Baked Trout

1 x 2½-3 lb trout
salt and pepper
1 onion, thinly sliced
pinch of dried sage or 2 fresh leaves
pinch of thyme or 1 fresh sprig
2-3 rashers bacon

Clean the trout and place salt and pepper, onion, sage and thyme inside cavity. Arrange bacon rashers over the fish and place on a large piece of greased, doubled aluminium foil. Wrap fish securely and cook on barbecue over medium hot coals for approximately 1-1¼ hours or until fish flakes easily with a fork. Turn occasionally while cooking.

Bouillabaisse

SERVES: 6-8

3 lb fish fillets, a selection of bream, snapper and
  jewfish (or bream, haddock and bass)
1 small crayfish (or lobster)
$\frac{1}{2}$ cup olive oil
4 carrots, thinly sliced
2 onions, thinly sliced
4 cloves garlic, crushed
2 leeks, thinly sliced
4 large tomatoes
bouquet garni (thyme, bay leaf, parsley, celery,
  rosemary)
4 large potatoes, sliced
3 cups fish stock, made from fish trimmings
$\frac{1}{2}$ teaspoon powdered saffron
salt
freshly ground pepper
24 fresh mussels in shells

Cut fish into 2-inch pieces. Remove meat from crayfish,
cut into chunks.
Heat oil in a large heavy based saucepan or flameproof
casserole. Add carrots, onions, garlic and leeks, sauté until
golden brown. Chop tomatoes and add to pan with the
bouquet garni.
Add pieces of fish and potato to pan, cook for
approximately 5 minutes, stir gently. Add fish stock and
seasonings and bring to the boil. Simmer for 15 minutes.
Add mussels and crayfish meat and cook just until mussels
open.
Serve Bouillabaisse as 2 courses. The soup followed by the
fish and potatoes.

Fish Fillets with Parsley Sauce

SERVES: 6

1 teaspoon salt
freshly ground pepper
2 tablespoons salad oil
2 lb fish fillets, flathead (or whiting)
2 tablespoons French mustard
2 oz butter or margarine, softened
$\frac{1}{4}$ cup finely chopped parsley
$\frac{1}{4}$ cup lemon juice
extra $\frac{1}{2}$ teaspoon salt

Add salt and pepper to oil, rub mixture over fish fillets.
Barbecue over medium coals for approximately 10-15
minutes or until fillets are lightly browned on both sides,
remove from barbecue.
Combine remaining ingredients and mix together
thoroughly. Spread half the mixture over fish.
Return fish to barbecue until sizzling and fish flakes easily
with a fork.
Serve with remaining savoury butter.

Grilled Fish Steaks

SERVES: 4

4 fish steaks, jewfish (or halibut)
1 teaspoon salt
$\frac{1}{4}$ teaspoon pepper
2 oz butter or margarine, melted
1 tablespoon lemon juice
1 teaspoon finely chopped chervil leaves
Avocado Sauce (see page 94)

Sprinkle fish with salt and pepper. Combine melted butter, lemon juice and chervil and brush over fish.
Place fish steaks in greased wire grill and barbecue over medium coals turning once while cooking. Barbecue for approximately 10-15 minutes or until fish flakes easily with a fork. Baste with lemon butter when cooking is completed. Serve fish with Avocado Sauce.

Herbed Grilled Fish

1 x 1½-2 lb fish, bream (or bluefish)
fresh fennel, dill or thyme
Sauce:
4 oz butter, melted
1 teaspoon salt
freshly ground pepper
1 teaspoon ground coriander seed
¼ teaspoon cardamon
2 tablespoons lemon juice
1 cup yoghurt

Wash and dry fish. Brush fish inside and out with the sauce.
Place in a greased wire grill.
Barbecue over medium coals for approximately 30-45
minutes or until fish is lightly brown on both sides and
flakes easily with a fork. Turn frequently and baste
occasionally with the sauce while cooking.
Before removing fish from barbecue, place fresh herbs on
coals, the smouldering herbs will flavour the fish.
Heat any remaining sauce and serve with the fish.
Sauce: Combine all ingredients and mix together thoroughly.

Sole en Papillote

SERVES: 4

1 lb fillets of sole
1 teaspoon salt
½ cup thinly sliced mushrooms
1 oz butter or margarine
1 cup dry sherry
1 tablespoon finely chopped onion
1 tablespoon (½ oz) cornflour
⅓ cup cold water
2 tablespoons lemon juice
8 oz prawns (or shrimp), shelled
1 tablespoon finely chopped parsley

Divide fish into 4 portions and sprinkle with salt.
Sauté mushrooms in butter until tender, add sherry and
onion. Blend cornflour with water until smooth, add to
mushrooms and stirring continuously, bring to the boil.
Simmer for 1 minute, add lemon juice.
Place each portion of sole on a piece of greased, doubled
aluminium foil, cover with prawns. Turn foil up around fish
and pour sauce over the top. Sprinkle with parsley and
wrap fish securely.
Cook over medium hot coals for approximately 20 minutes,
or until fish flakes easily with a fork.

Whiting with Almonds

4 whole whiting
2 tablespoons (1 oz) plain flour
$\frac{1}{2}$ teaspoon salt
freshly ground pepper
4 oz butter or margarine, melted
2 oz slivered almonds
$\frac{1}{4}$ cup lemon juice

Wash and dry fish thoroughly. Combine flour, salt and pepper, roll fish in seasoned flour. Place fish in a greased wire grill.

Barbecue over medium coals for approximately 20 minutes or until fish flakes easily with a fork, turn frequently while cooking and baste occasionally with 2 oz butter.

Pour remaining butter in a small saucepan, heat and add almonds, stir occasionally until almonds are golden brown, add lemon juice.

Place barbecued fish on a warm serving plate and pour sauce over.

Note: Whiting may also be cooked in a heavy based frying pan or skillet over barbecue.

Barbecued Crayfish

SERVES: 2-4

1 large green crayfish (or lobster)
4 oz butter or margarine, melted
$\frac{1}{3}$ cup lemon juice
salt and pepper
1 clove garlic, crushed (optional)

Break crayfish in half and split the tail down the centre.
Combine butter, lemon juice, salt and pepper and garlic,
mix together thoroughly.
Place crayfish tail, shell side down, on barbecue over
medium coals, baste generously with lemon butter.
Barbecue crayfish for approximately 5 minutes, baste again,
turn and cook for 2 minutes.
Continue to barbecue crayfish in this way, 5 minutes on
the shell side, 2 minutes on the meat side until crayfish
has been cooked for approximately 15-20 minutes in all.
When crayfish meat is white and the shell is bright red, the
crayfish is cooked, serve immediately.
Warm any remaining lemon butter and serve with the
crayfish.

Charcoal Grilled Prawns

SERVES: 4-6

2 lb green prawns (or shrimp), shelled and deveined
Marinade:
1 cup olive oil
¼ cup lemon juice
½ cup finely chopped onion
2 cloves garlic, crushed
¼ cup finely chopped parsley

Place prawns in a bowl, add marinade and mix well. Cover and stand for several hours. Drain prawns.
Place in a heavy based frying pan or skillet and cook over medium coals for approximately 10-15 minutes or until cooked. Stir frequently and add a little marinade while cooking.
Serve immediately.
Marinade: Combine all ingredients and mix together thoroughly.

Seafood Kebabs

SERVES: 4-5

1 x 2 lb green crayfish (or lobster)
8 oz green prawns (or shrimp)
8 oz fresh scallops
small tomatoes
large stuffed green olives
salt and pepper
2 oz butter, melted
2 tablespoons lemon juice
2 tablespoons finely chopped parsley

Remove meat from tail of crayfish, cut into chunks. Shell and devein prawns. Alternate crayfish, prawns, scallops, tomatoes and olives onto skewers. Sprinkle with salt and pepper. Combine melted butter and lemon juice and brush over the kebabs.
Barbecue over medium coals for approximately 10-15 minutes, turn frequently.
Baste with lemon butter and sprinkle with parsley before serving.

Vegetables, Salads and Breads

Here are a selection of accompaniments for barbecued fish, meat and poultry. Vegetables which can be cooked on the barbecue, amongst them, Ratatouille and Barbecued Baked Beans which are perfect served with barbecued chops and steaks. There are also delicious salads and hot breads to serve with your next barbecued meal.

Top, Clockwise:
Tossed Green Salad
Bacon Onion Rolls
Barbecued Sausages
Barbecued T-Bone Steaks
Tomatoes Vinaigrette
Barbecued Baked Beans

Baked Potatoes

For each serving:

1 potato
1 tablespoon salad oil
salt and pepper

Choose firm, even sized potatoes, scrub well and dry. Prick
with a fork, brush with oil and sprinkle with salt and
pepper. Wrap each potato separately in a piece of
aluminium foil.
Barbecue over hot coals or directly in the coals for
approximately 45 minutes-1 hour or until tender. Turn
potatoes occasionally while cooking.
Serve with butter, sour cream mixed with chopped chives
or cream cheese mixed with chopped parsley and salt and
pepper.
Note: Onions may be cooked in the same way.

Barbecued Baked Beans

SERVES: 4

1 oz butter or margarine
4 oz bacon pieces, chopped
$\frac{1}{4}$ cup chopped celery
$\frac{1}{4}$ cup chopped onion
1 x 16 oz can baked beans
1 tablespoon horseradish relish
1 teaspoon French mustard

Melt butter in a heavy based saucepan or fireproof
casserole and add bacon, celery and onion. Cook gently,
stirring occasionally until ingredients are golden brown.
Add remaining ingredients, stir well, cover and cook gently
on barbecue over medium coals for approximately 20
minutes or until baked beans are hot.
Serve with barbecued frankfurters and sausages.

Whiting with Almonds

Corn on the Cob

Allow 1 corn cob for each person. Select young, tender corn cobs. Turn back husks and strip off silk. Brush corn with melted butter or margarine and sprinkle with salt and freshly ground pepper. Replace the husks and secure in 3 places with thin florist's wire.

Barbecue corn cobs over hot coals for approximately 15-20 minutes, or until tender, turn frequently. When cooked, husks will be dry and brown and corn will be golden brown. Serve with melted butter and salt and pepper.

Variation: After stripping off silk, wrap a derinded bacon rasher around each corn cob and secure at the ends with cocktail sticks. Replace the husks and proceed as above.

Note: Husks may be removed from corn cobs completely and after brushing corn with melted butter and seasoning with salt and pepper, wrap individually in aluminium foil and barbecue over hot coals for approximately 20 minutes or until tender. Serve as above.

Glazed Carrots

Select small tender carrots, scrub well. Place in boiling salted water and cook until almost tender, drain thoroughly. Place on barbecue over hot coals and brush with melted butter or margarine and sprinkle with a little ground coriander seed. Barbecue carrots for approximately 5-7 minutes, turning frequently and basting with melted butter as they cook.

Glazed Pineapple Rings

SERVES: 6-8

6-8 fresh or canned pineapple rings
Glaze:
½ cup honey
1 tablespoon French mustard

Barbecue pineapple over medium hot coals for approximately 5-7 minutes or until lightly browned. Baste frequently with the glaze while cooking.
Serve with barbecued frankfurters and sausages.
Glaze: Mix honey and mustard together.

Grilled Mushrooms

SERVES: 4

1 lb mushrooms
2 oz butter or margarine
salt and pepper

Wash and trim mushrooms, slice if large. Divide into 4
portions and place each on a piece of doubled aluminium
foil. Dot with butter and sprinkle lightly with salt and
pepper.
Wrap mushrooms securely and barbecue over hot coals for
approximately 15-20 minutes or until mushrooms are
tender, turn occasionally while cooking.
Serve with barbecued steak.

Rice Pilaf

SERVES: 4

3 oz butter or margarine
1 cup long grain rice
1 clove garlic, crushed
$2\frac{1}{2}$-3 cups beef stock or water and 2 beef stock cubes
$\frac{1}{4}$ cup chopped ham
2 tablespoons flaked almonds, toasted
salt and pepper

Heat butter in heavy based frying pan, add rice and garlic.
Stir until rice begins to colour. Remove from heat and add
stock. Cover pan and cook over medium coals for
approximately 30 minutes or until rice is tender. Add
additional stock if rice appears to be dry. The liquid should
be absorbed by the time the rice is tender. Remove pan
from heat and add ham and almonds. Stir lightly with a
fork, season to taste with salt and pepper and serve
immediately.
Ideal accompaniment for kebabs.

Ratatouille

SERVES: 6-8

4 tablespoons olive oil
2 cloves garlic, crushed
1 lb eggplant, thinly sliced
2 lb tomatoes, thinly sliced
1 lb zucchini, thinly sliced
4 green peppers, seeded and thinly sliced
1 cup white wine or water
salt and pepper

Heat oil and garlic in a large heavy based frying pan or
skillet and brown vegetables in turn, cooking quickly and
placing them into a deep, flameproof casserole as they
brown (add extra olive oil to pan if necessary). When all
the vegetables are browned, pour wine over and add salt
and pepper to taste.
Simmer on barbecue for approximately 1 hour or until
vegetables are tender. Do not stir.
Serve hot as a vegetable accompaniment or cold as an
hors d'oeuvre.

Coleslaw

SERVES: 6

4 cups shredded cabbage
$\frac{1}{2}$ cup finely chopped cucumber
$\frac{1}{2}$ cup finely chopped celery
$\frac{1}{4}$ cup finely chopped green pepper
Dressing:
$\frac{3}{4}$ **cup mayonnaise**
3 tablespoons vinegar
1 teaspoon French mustard
$\frac{1}{4}$ **teaspoon paprika pepper**
$\frac{1}{4}$ **teaspoon salt**

Combine prepared vegetables in a salad bowl, chill. Pour dressing over and toss together gently, adjust seasoning if necessary.
Dressing: Combine all ingredients and mix together thoroughly.

86

French Bean Salad

SERVES: 6

1½ lb French beans
1 small onion, finely chopped
¼ cup slivered almonds, toasted
French dressing (see page 105)

Top and tail beans, string and cut diagonally into 2-inch pieces. Cook in boiling salted water for approximately 10-15 minutes or just until tender, drain and cool. Place beans in salad bowl, add onion and just before serving, add slivered almonds and pour over French dressing. Toss together gently and serve immediately.

Tossed Green Salad

SERVES: 4-6

1 large lettuce
1 cucumber, peeled and thinly sliced
4 shallots, sliced
1 green pepper, seeded and sliced
French dressing (see page 105)

Wash lettuce well, drain and chill until crisp, tear into bite size pieces. Place all vegetables in salad bowl, pour over French dressing just before serving and toss salad lightly.

Sour Cream Potato Salad

SERVES: 8

2 lb potatoes, peeled
$\frac{1}{3}$ cup French dressing (see page 105)
$\frac{1}{2}$ cup finely chopped cucumber
$\frac{1}{2}$ cup finely chopped celery
$\frac{1}{4}$ cup thinly sliced onion
4 hard-boiled eggs, coarsely chopped
1 cup mayonnaise
$\frac{1}{2}$ cup sour cream
1 tablespoon horseradish relish
salt
freshly ground pepper
2 rashers bacon, cooked and crumbled, for garnish

Cook potatoes in boiling salted water until just tender.
Drain well and cut into $\frac{1}{2}$-inch cubes. Place potato in a
bowl and pour over the French dressing while potatoes are
still warm. When cool, add cucumber, celery, onion and
egg. Mix mayonnaise, sour cream and horseradish relish
together and pour over salad. Toss together gently and
season to taste with salt and pepper.
Garnish with bacon just before serving.

Tomatoes Vinaigrette

SERVES: 6

2 lb firm red tomatoes
1 onion, finely chopped
2 tablespoons dried basil
½ cup finely chopped parsley
⅓ cup French dressing (see page 105)

Wash and slice tomatoes. Place in layers in a salad bowl, sprinkling each layer with onion, basil and parsley. Pour French dressing over salad and marinate for 2 hours before serving.

Hot Garlic Bread

1 loaf French bread
4 oz butter or margarine, softened
1 large clove garlic, crushed

Cut bread diagonally into 1-inch slices, cutting to, but not through, the bottom crust.

Cream butter with crushed garlic, spread between slices.

Press loaf firmly together. Wrap in aluminium foil and seal securely.

Heat on barbecue over medium coals for approximately 20 minutes, turn loaf once. Serve when butter has melted and bread is hot. Open foil and cut through bottom crust just before serving.

Variations:

Anchovy: Omit garlic. Soak 6 anchovy fillets in milk for 30 minutes. Drain and chop finely, add to butter with 1 teaspoon anchovy sauce.

Herb cheese: Cream 2 teaspoons finely chopped parsley, $\frac{1}{2}$ teaspoon finely chopped oregano leaves and 2 tablespoons grated Parmesan cheese with the garlic butter.

Herb lemon: Omit garlic. Cream 2 teaspoons lemon juice, 1 tablespoon finely chopped fresh herbs and pinch of salt with butter.

Onion: Omit garlic. Cream 2 tablespoons finely chopped onion or chives with butter.

Seeds: Omit garlic. Cream 1-2 teaspoons of celery, poppy, dill or sesame seeds with butter.

Bacon Onion Rolls

SERVES: 6

6 bread rolls
2 oz butter
2 tablespoons salad oil
2 large onions, finely chopped
6 rashers bacon, derinded and finely chopped

Split bread rolls and butter.
Heat oil in heavy based frying pan or skillet and fry onion and bacon together until golden brown. Place mixture in rolls and wrap securely in pieces of aluminium foil.
Place on barbecue over medium coals for approximately 15 minutes or until hot, turn occasionally. Serve immediately.

Italian Sandwich

1 loaf French bread
2 oz butter or margarine
1 clove garlic, crushed
2 tomatoes, thinly sliced
4 oz Cheddar cheese, thinly sliced
4 oz corned beef or ham, thinly sliced
1 green pepper, seeded and cut into rings

Cut bread diagonally into 1-inch slices, cutting to, but not through, the bottom crust.
Cream butter with garlic, spread between slices. Place a slice of tomato, cheese, meat and green pepper between each slice of bread. Press loaf firmly together again.
Wrap in aluminium foil and place on barbecue over medium coals for approximately 20-25 minutes or until cheese begins to melt and bread is hot. Turn loaf once while heating.
To serve, remove foil and cut through bottom crust of loaf.

91

Sauces, Marinades and Relishes

Sauces, Marinades and Relishes

Tasty piquant sauces served with barbecued meats, fish and poultry provide a variety of flavours to grilled food. Some are basted over food while it is being barbecued, others are served at the table when cooking is completed. There are marinades to tenderize and add flavour to meat. Use small heavy based saucepans when making sauces on the barbecue. Sauces for basting can be placed in fireproof pots and kept close at hand by the barbecue. These recipes will add originality to your barbecue menus.

Almond Sauce

4 oz butter or margarine
2 oz slivered almonds
salt
freshly ground pepper
pinch of nutmeg
2 teaspoons lemon juice
2 tablespoons finely chopped chives

Melt butter in a saucepan and add almonds, cook gently until almonds are golden brown. Add seasonings and lemon juice. Before serving, add chives and mix together thoroughly.
Serve with barbecued chicken.

Avocado Sauce

1 ripe avocado pear
$\frac{1}{2}$ cup sour cream
1 teaspoon lemon juice
$\frac{1}{4}$ teaspoon salt
freshly ground pepper
few drops Tabasco sauce

Peel avocado pear, remove stone and mash with a fork in a mixing bowl. Add remaining ingredients and mix together thoroughly.
Serve with barbecued shellfish.

Barbecue Sauce

1 oz butter or margarine
1¼ cups finely chopped onion
2 tablespoons (1 oz) brown sugar
1 tablespoon vinegar
1 tablespoon Worcestershire sauce
½ cup tomato sauce
¼ cup water
2 tablespoons lemon juice

Melt butter in saucepan and add finely chopped onion,
sauté until golden. Add remaining ingredients and bring to
the boil, simmer for 15 minutes.
Serve with barbecued sausages, frankfurters and
hamburgers.

Barbecue Wine Sauce

1 small onion, finely chopped
1 clove garlic, crushed
1 cup red wine
$\frac{1}{2}$ cup water
$\frac{1}{2}$ cup olive oil
$\frac{1}{4}$ cup red wine vinegar
1 teaspoon Worcestershire sauce
$\frac{1}{2}$ teaspoon chilli sauce
1 teaspoon sugar
2 teaspoons French mustard
1 teaspoon salt
1 teaspoon paprika pepper
$\frac{1}{4}$ teaspoon Tabasco sauce

Place all ingredients in a saucepan and bring to the boil.
Simmer for 5 minutes, strain and cool.
Use to marinate and baste meat.

Top, Left to Right:
Green Pepper Sauce
Redcurrant Glaze
Barbecue Wine Sauce
Teriyaki Marinade
Tomato Sauce
Basting Sauce for Lamb
Horseradish Sauce
Satay Sauce

Basting Sauce for Lamb

3 tablespoons olive oil
2 tablespoons white wine
$\frac{1}{2}$ teaspoon finely chopped fresh thyme
2 teaspoons finely chopped mint
$\frac{1}{2}$ teaspoon salt
freshly ground pepper

Combine all ingredients and mix together thoroughly.
Suitable for using as a marinade or basting sauce for any
lamb dish.

Green Pepper Sauce

1 onion, finely chopped
2 green peppers, seeded and finely chopped
$\frac{1}{2}$ oz butter or margarine
4 tablespoons water
2 tomatoes, chopped
salt and pepper
$\frac{1}{4}$ teaspoon chilli sauce

Sauté onion and peppers in butter in a saucepan until
golden brown. Add remaining ingredients, bring to the boil
and simmer gently for 10 minutes. Adjust seasoning if
necessary.
Serve hot with barbecued meats.

Barbecued Chicken Halves

Horseradish Sauce

½ oz butter or margarine
1 tablespoon (½ oz) plain flour
½ cup chicken stock or water and chicken stock cube
2 tablespoons horseradish relish
½ cup cream
pinch of cayenne pepper
salt and pepper

Melt the butter in a saucepan, add flour and blend together, cook for 2-3 minutes without colouring. Add stock and stirring continuously, bring to the boil, simmer for 3 minutes. Add remaining ingredients and season to taste with salt and pepper.
Serve hot with barbecued steak.

Peanut Sauce

1 onion, finely chopped
1 clove garlic, crushed
2 oz butter or margarine, melted
1 tablespoon soya sauce
3 tablespoons peanut butter
1 tablespoon lemon juice
½ cup cream

Sauté onion and garlic in butter in a saucepan until golden. Add soya sauce, peanut butter and lemon juice and mix together thoroughly, cool. Before serving, add the cream. Delicious served with barbecued steaks and chops.

Redcurrant Glaze

1 cup redcurrant jelly
1 x 6 fl oz can frozen concentrated orange juice
1 teaspoon dry mustard
pinch of ground ginger

Combine all ingredients in a saucepan and stirring
continuously, heat gently until smooth.
Baste chickens with glaze while barbecuing.

Satay Sauce

1 onion, finely chopped
2 cloves garlic, crushed
2 tablespoons salad oil
1 cup dry white wine
$\frac{1}{4}$ cup dry sherry
$\frac{1}{4}$ cup soy sauce
2 tablespoons tomato purée
1 tablespoon peanut butter

Sauté onion and garlic in oil in a saucepan until golden.
Add wine, sherry, soy sauce and tomato purée. Bring to the
boil and simmer until reduced by a third. Add peanut butter
and mix thoroughly.
Use sauce to baste and serve with satays.

Teriyaki Marinade

$\frac{3}{4}$ cup canned pineapple juice
3 tablespoons soy sauce
3 tablespoons lemon juice
2 cloves garlic, crushed
1 bay leaf
pinch of ground cloves

Combine all ingredients in a screw-top jar, shake well.
Use to marinate meat immediately or store in refrigerator
until ready to use.

Tomato Sauce

4 large ripe tomatoes, skinned
4 tablespoons tomato ketchup
1 tablespoon red wine vinegar
2 tablespoons salad oil
2 drops Tabasco sauce
pinch of dry mustard
salt and pepper

Coarsely chop the tomatoes and mix with remaining
ingredients. Season to taste with salt and pepper.
Serve with barbecued sausages and chops.

Lemon Butter

4 oz butter or margarine
3 tablespoons lemon juice

Melt butter in a saucepan over medium heat until it foams
and becomes light brown. Remove from heat and add
lemon juice.
Use to baste and serve with barbecued fish and meat.

Fresh Chutney

1 apple
1 onion
3 tomatoes
3 stalks celery
1 cap pimiento
1 tablespoon finely chopped mint
1 tablespoon horseradish relish
1 clove garlic, crushed
2 tablespoons (1 oz) sugar
2 tablespoons vinegar
1 teaspoon salt
freshly ground pepper

Peel and grate the apple and onion. Skin the tomatoes and chop roughly. Finely chop the celery and pimiento. Place all ingredients in a saucepan and bring to the boil, simmer 4-5 minutes.
Serve hot or cold with grilled steak, chops, sausages and kebabs.

Apple and Mint Relish

1 large cooking apple
2 tablespoons apricot jam
1 tablespoon vinegar
1 tablespoon finely chopped mint
salt and pepper

Peel and grate the apple. Mix immediately with remaining ingredients in a mixing bowl, season to taste.
Serve relish with barbecued beef and lamb.

Anchovy Mayonnaise

2 teaspoons anchovy sauce
1¼ cups mayonnaise
1 tablespoon finely chopped parsley or capers
1 tablespoon chopped dill cucumber
1 clove garlic, crushed
3 black olives, stoned and chopped
1 hard-boiled egg, chopped
2 tablespoons cream
salt
freshly ground pepper

Combine all ingredients in a mixing bowl and mix together thoroughly, adjust seasoning if necessary.
Serve with barbecued fish.

French Dressing

3 parts salad oil
1 part vinegar
$\frac{1}{2}$ teaspoon salt
freshly ground pepper

Combine all ingredients together in a screw-top jar, shake
well. Store in refrigerator if not being used immediately.
Crushed garlic, French or English mustard or chopped herbs
may be added to the basic dressing.
Olive, safflower or peanut oil may be used.
There are a variety of vinegars to choose from, cider, red
wine, white wine and various vinegars flavoured with herbs.

Desserts and Drinks

Desserts and Drinks

What a delicious idea, barbecued desserts. Here are recipes for your next barbecue, everyone will love them. Children can make their own Fruit Kebabs while adults eat Fruit Flambées, a wonderful finale to a meal eaten out of doors.

Make a large jug of ice cold Cider Cup or Sangria when the weather is hot or try Mulled Wine in the cooler months, your party will be off to a swinging start.

106

Baked Apples

SERVES: 6

6 cooking apples
$\frac{1}{2}$ cup (3 oz) brown sugar
$\frac{1}{4}$ cup chopped walnuts
$\frac{1}{4}$ cup chopped raisins
1 teaspoon ground cinnamon
1 oz butter or margarine
whipped cream for serving

Core apples and score skin around the middle. Combine
sugar, walnuts, raisins and cinnamon in a mixing bowl,
mix together thoroughly. Place each apple on a piece of
doubled aluminium foil, stuff with the mixture and dot with
butter.
Wrap securely in foil and place on barbecue over medium
hot coals for approximately 30-45 minutes or until tender.
Turn once while cooking.
Serve with whipped cream.

Banana Delight

For each serving:

1 banana
4 marshmallows
1 oz dark cooking chocolate, chopped

Peel banana and cut in half lengthways. Cut marshmallows in halves with scissors. Place banana on a piece of aluminium foil, cover with marshmallows and chocolate. Seal foil firmly and place on barbecue over hot coals for 10-15 minutes, or until banana is tender and marshmallows and chocolate melt.
Serve in foil packages.
Note: This sweet is ideal for children's barbecue parties.

Fruit Flambées

Pineapple, peaches and strawberries are all ideal.
Insert stainless steel skewers through whole pineapple and
place on barbecue over hot coals and when warmed
through, remove skin and cut into chunks. Place fruit on a
metal tray, heavy based frying pan or skillet, sprinkle with
brown sugar and rum. Warm over fire again, ignite and
serve flaming.
Peel, halve and stone fresh freestone peaches, fill cavity
with brown sugar and rum or brandy. Place on barbecue
over hot coals until warmed through. Place on a metal tray,
heavy based frying pan or skillet, pour over more rum or
brandy and ignite. Serve flaming.
Place strawberries on a metal tray, heavy based frying pan
or skillet, sprinkle with brown sugar and rum or brandy,
heat over barbecue, ignite and serve flaming.
Note: At buffet parties, place cocktail sticks in piece of
fruit before serving.

Fruit Kebabs

Cut chunks of pineapple, apple, peach, apricot and banana.
Whole strawberries and large grapes are also suitable.
Thread fruit onto skewers. Brush with melted butter and
sprinkle with sugar or baste with a mixture of brown sugar,
lemon juice and orange juice.
Barbecue over hot coals, turn frequently. Baste again and
serve when fruit is still slightly crisp and sugar has
caramelized.

Hawaiian Oranges

For each serving:

1 orange
1 tablespoon ($\frac{1}{2}$ oz) brown sugar
pinch of cinnamon
1 tablespoon rum
$\frac{1}{4}$ oz butter or margarine
whipped cream or ice cream for serving

Peel orange and separate into segments. Place on a piece of aluminium foil. Turn sides of foil up, sprinkle with sugar, cinnamon and rum and dot with butter.
Wrap securely in foil and place on barbecue over hot coals for approximately 15 minutes. Turn once while cooking.
Serve with whipped cream or ice cream.

Peaches Italienne

SERVES: 6

12 canned peach halves, drained
6 tablespoons sherry
$\frac{1}{3}$ cup slivered almonds, toasted
ice cream or whipped cream for serving

Place 2 peach halves on each piece of aluminium foil.
Turn sides of foil up and pour 1 tablespoon of sherry over
each serving.
Seal foil firmly and place on barbecue over hot coals for
approximately 10 minutes or until peaches are warm.
To serve, remove peaches from foil packages, sprinkle with
slivered almonds and serve with ice cream or whipped
cream.

Cider Cup

SERVES: 6-8

ice cubes
grated rind of 1 lemon
5 cups cider
1 tablespoon maraschino
1 tablespoon curaçao
1 tablespoon brandy
3 cups soda water

Place ice cubes and grated lemon rind in a large jug. Add
remaining ingredients, mix well and serve immediately.

Fruit Punch

SERVES: 14-16

1 cup (8 oz) sugar
1 cup water
2 cups canned pineapple juice
1 cup orange juice
juice of 1 lemon
5 cups cold weak tea
$2\frac{1}{2}$ cups ginger ale
2 passionfruit
sprigs of mint
6 strawberries, chopped
crushed ice

Place sugar and water in a saucepan over gentle heat. Stir
until sugar is dissolved, boil for 2-3 minutes. Cool and
add fruit juices and tea. Chill well and just before serving
add cold ginger ale, passionfruit pulp, sprigs of mint,
strawberries and crushed ice.
Serve in chilled glasses.

Banana Delight

112

Mulled Wine

SERVES: 6-8

2½ cups red wine, claret or Burgundy
2 tablespoons brandy
1 tablespoon gin
4 lumps sugar
juice of 2 oranges
juice of 1 lemon
2 cups soda water
ice cubes
thin slices of orange and lemon for garnish

Place all ingredients except soda water, ice cubes and
sliced fruit in a large jug. Mix thoroughly and place in
refrigerator to chill, stir occasionally.
When ready to serve, add soda water, ice cubes and sliced
fruit.

Sangria

SERVES: 4

2½ cups red wine, claret or Burgundy
juice of ½ lemon
3 cloves
2 tablespoons (1 oz) castor sugar
stick of cinnamon

Place all ingredients in a saucepan. Bring to the boil and
simmer for 2-3 minutes, stirring continuously.
Strain and serve.

Baked Apple

The
Barbecue

The Barbecue

To barbecue is to roast over an open fire. With a little thought and preparation, almost any meat or fish which can be cooked in an oven, can be barbecued.

114

Barbecues and Equipment:
There are innumerable barbecues to choose from. Consider them all carefully and choose a design which suits your particular needs. Undoubtedly, the most versatile barbecue to choose is a portable one. At home, it can be placed in the best possible position, depending on the elements. It can also be dismantled simply and packed into the car to use else-where. Choose a design which gives the cook the opportunity to barbecue either 'upwind' or 'downwind'. Locate your barbecue in a spot where any breeze will blow smoke away from the eating area. Always select an area a safe distance from shrubs, trees and dry grass, this is particularly important when building a bush barbecue.

Basically, very little barbecue equipment is essential, but some items certainly make barbecuing easier. Ensure that the items you buy are sturdy in design and will stand up to a certain amount of rough treatment! A long-handled pair of tongs and fork are basic necessities and a sturdy oven mit to protect the cook's hand is a good idea. Skewers are essentail for testing foods and for barbecuing kebabs. These are made in various metals, stainless steel being extremely popular and practical. There are also shorter bamboo varieties which are ideal for seafood appetizers and fruit kebabs served as a dessert. Select bristle brushes for basting food. Small paint brushes are suitable, but do not choose any plastic or nylon varieties. Marinades, oils and melted butter can be kept in fireproof pots by the barbecue. Hinged wire grills are essential when grilling over a bush barbecue as they can be turned easily when holding a number of chops, fish, frank-furters or hamburgers. Long-handled cast iron pots of various sizes, frying pans and skillets are handy for heating sauces, hotpots, frying fish and various meats. When buying plates, cutlery, glassware and table linen for barbecue parties, choose those which are sturdy and easy to look after. Bright colours promote a gay, casual atmosphere.

Aluminium foil is an extremely handy commodity when barbecuing. It can be used for wrapping potatoes, vegetables, bread, meat and fish. Use double foil to give extra strength and if foods to be barbecued are dry, grease foil with butter or oil. Food wrapped in foil may be placed directly in low coals or may be placed on grill or hotplate above hot coals. Wrap food in one of the following ways:

Tent wrap: Tear off desired length of aluminium foil. Place food to be wrapped in centre and bring two opposite edges together loosely across the top. Make a double or triple sealed edge, leaving enough room above and around the sides of the food for air to circulate freely. Triple fold ends flat. Food is thus wrapped in a loose wrap.

Bag wrap: Place food on a piece of aluminium foil. Bring all sides of foil up around food and seal by pressing all sides together by twisting top to close.

Building and Lighting your Fire:

There are many theories as to the best method of starting a fire. Ease and quickness are essential factors. Charcoal, available in lump or briquette form, is definitely the quickest and easiest fuel to use in a barbecue. Certain types of dry, slow burning woods make good long-lasting coals and give a delicious flavour to barbecued foods.

When using wood, remember the fire must be prepared and lit well in advance so that by the time the barbecue is required for cooking, there are plenty of hot coals.

When using charcoal in your barbecue, soak a quantity of charcoal in methylated spirits for approximately three hours before the barbecue is to be lit. Place a layer of soaked charcoal in the barbecue then a layer of unsoaked charcoal on top. Alternatively, place charcoal to a depth of approximately two inches in the barbecue. On top, spaced approximately six inches apart, place firelighters (available at leading stores). Light fire and in approximately 45 minutes, when charcoal is covered with grey ash by day time or glows at night time, cooking may commence. Never use petrol or kerosine to help you light your fire.

For a bush barbecue, light the fire with paper, dry twigs and leaves. Add larger pieces of wood to the fire as it becomes established. Barbecuing may commence in approximately two hours or when there are plenty of hot glowing coals and the flames have disappeared. Once your fire is established, disturb it as little as possible. Constant poking and raking breaks up pockets of heat and lowers the temperature of the fire.

Use your hand to judge the heat of your fire. Hold your hand, palm towards the heat, near the grill level. If you have to withdraw your hand in less than three seconds, the coals are hot (approximately 400°F). If you can keep your hand at that level for three to four seconds, the coals are medium (approximately 350°F). For low coals (approximately 300°F), you should be able to keep your hand at grill level for four to five seconds.

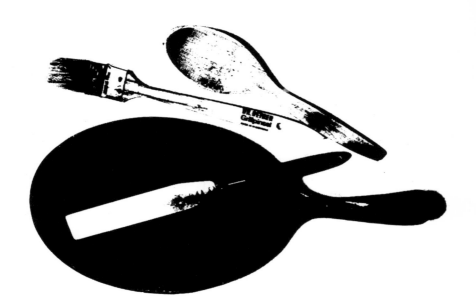

Cooking on the Barbecue:
The most important thing to remember when barbecuing is to
barbecue with heat, not flames. The heat must be controlled
so that the food is evenly cooked, not charred on the outside
and raw inside.
Barbecue food ten to sixteen inches away from the coals.
Once the fire is evenly alight and ready for barbecuing,
the heat may be controlled by the use of a hose fitted
with a pressure reduction valve which gives a fine spray.
This reduces the temperature of the fire quickly and cuts
charcoal wastage. The water also prevents fat from food, such
as sausages and steaks, from falling into the fire—this would
accelerate the combustion of the charcoal and would be
likely to burn the food being cooked. If the top of cooking
food is sprayed with a fine spray of water, the globules of fat
and water combine and explode into flame before touching
the charcoal. It is a most effective way of controlling heat
when barbecuing. Small pieces of food can be barbecued
efficiently when this method is adopted. On the other hand,
if more heat is required quickly when barbecuing, throw a few
pieces of fat from the trimmed meat onto the charcoal or
baste food with a little melted butter or oil, the dripping fat
will activate the fire. When barbecuing is almost completed,
try throwing a few gum leaves or herbs on the fire, it will give
the food a delicious flavour.

119

Tips for Successful Barbecuing:
- When a new barbecue has been purchased, read the manufacturer's instructions carefully before using. There may be certain tips which will be helpful.
- Many people line the firebox with doubled aluminium foil which reflects heat back to the food and therefore quickens cooking time. The foil also keeps your equipment clean.
- Vary the size of your fire depending on the amount of food to be cooked. Only make a small shallow fire to barbecue one steak or a few chops.
- Marinating meat before barbecuing adds flavour to your meat. It also tenderizes cheaper cuts of meat.
- Trim most fat from meat before barbecuing to prevent fat drippings from making the fire flare while cooking. Remaining fat should be snipped at regular intervals to prevent edges of meat from curling while cooking.
- Do not baste food with butter or oil while barbecuing as flames will burn the cooking food. Baste before and after the food is cooked.
- Use fat trimmed from meat for greasing hot plates and wire grills, this prevents meat from sticking.
- Aluminium foil trays and pans are handy for barbecues. Food can be kept warm in them, can be cooked in them or they can be used as serving dishes.

Terms used in Barbecue Cookbook

Baste:
: To moisten food while cooking with fat, oil or a special sauce or marinade to prevent drying and to add flavour.

Chilli Sauce:
: A hot pepper sauce, not to be confused with the milder chili sauce.

Cornflour:
: Cornstarch.

Grill:
: To broil—to cook by direct heat over hot coals.

Marinate:
: To stand food in a liquid for a certain length of time to add flavour, or, as in the case of some meats, to tenderize.

Minced Steak:
: Ground beef.

Sear:
: To brown outer surface of meat very quickly by intense heat. It improves the appearance of the meat and keeps the flavour and meat juices inside.

Score:
: To cut narrow grooves or gashes part way through the outer surface of food.

Shallot:
: Spring onion.

Truss:
: To tie chicken with string or strong thread laced around metal skewers to hold its shape while cooking.

Acknowledgements

The editor would like to thank the following for their assistance in providing information and equipment for the Barbecue Cookbook.

Comalco Limited
David Jones'
Grace Bros. Pty. Ltd.
The Bay Tree Kitchen Shop, Woollahra
Gerry Kearney
Maurice Tattersall
    Head Teacher, Food School, Meat Division,
    East Sydney Technical College.

INDEX